Robbie Ravenbeak

Plays by Steve Barlow and Steve Skidmore

Illustrated by Connah Brecon

Contents

Published by Pearson Education Limited, Edinburgh Gate, Harlow, Essex, CM20 2JE.

www.pearsonschools.co.uk

Text © Steve Barlow and Steve Skidmore 2013
Designed by Sara Rafferty
Original illustrations © Connah Brecon 2013
Illustrated by Connah Brecon, The Bright Agency

The rights of Steve Barlow and Steve Skidmore to be identified as authors of this work have been asserted by them in accordance with the Copyright, Designs and Patents Act 1988.

First published 2013

21

10 9

British Library Cataloguing in Publication Data
A catalogue record for this book is available from the British Library

ISBN 978 0 435 14428 9

Printed and bound in the UK by Ashford Colour Press Ltd.

Acknowledgements

We would like to thank Bangor Central Integrated Primary School, Northern Ireland; Bishop Henderson Church of England Primary School, Somerset; Bletchingdon Parochial Church of England Primary School, Oxfordshire; Brookside Community Primary School, Somerset; Bude Park Primary School, Hull; Carisbrooke Church of England Primary School, Isle of Wight; Cheddington Combined School, Buckinghamshire; Dair House Independent School, Buckinghamshire; Deal Parochial School, Kent; Glebe Infant School, Goucestershire; Henley Green Primary School, Coventry; Lovelace Primary School, Surrey; Our Lady of Peace Junior School, Slough; Tackley Church of England Primary School, Oxfordshire; and Twyford Church of England School, Buckinghamshire for their invaluable help in the development and trialling of the Bug Club resources.

Every effort has been made to contact copyright holders of material reproduced in this book. Any omissions will be rectified in subsequent printings if notice is given to the publishers.

First Day At School

Characters

Mrs Brookes

a teacher

Robbie Ravenbeak

a Viking boy

Pupils at West Street School

Martin

Megan

Ellie

Sam

In the Classroom

Mrs Brookes and Robbie enter.

Mrs Brookes: Pencils down, everyone. I want you to meet Robbie.

Martin, Ellie and Megan: Hello, Robbie.

Sam: I don't believe it! He's a Viking!

Robbie growls.

Robbie: Aaaargh!

Ellie: Ooer.

Martin: He looks a bit fierce.

Megan: He's got an axe!

Mrs Brookes: Er … perhaps I'd better look after your axe until home time, Robbie.

Robbie glares at her, but hands it over.

Sam is scared.

Sam: He doesn't f-f-frighten me!

Mrs Brookes: Robbie, you can sit next to Sam.

Sam: Awww, Miss. Why does he have to sit with us?

Ellie: Oh, come on, Sam.

Megan: He's **new**.

Martin: Yeah, give him a chance.

Sam sulks.

Sam: He might interfere with my learning.

Robbie turns to Sam.

Robbie: Do you know what Vikings do to their enemies?

Sam looks nervous.

Sam: No, what?

Robbie whispers to Sam and Sam responds quickly.

Sam: Why don't you sit here?

Mrs Brookes: Let's all make Robbie feel welcome. Now, what were we doing before I went out?

Ellie: Maths, Miss.

Martin: You put these three cakes on the table …

Megan: … And you said, if you cut each of them in half, how many pieces would there be?

Mrs Brookes: Does anyone know what the answer is?

Martin: No, Miss.

Megan: Sorry.

Ellie: Seventeen – no, that can't be right …

Sam: None, because I'd eat them all!

Mrs Brookes: Don't be silly, Sam. How about you, Robbie?

Robbie tears the cakes in half with his bare hands.

Robbie: One-two-three-four-five-six!

Mrs Brookes looks nervous.

Mrs Brookes: Very good, Robbie ... but we don't usually use our hands. You'd better go and wash them now, dear.

Robbie goes to wash his hands.

Mrs Brookes: I think perhaps we need to practise working together, children.

Sam: Oh no!

Mrs Brookes: Now, Martin. If you and Ellie both went to pick up the same table tennis bat, how would you decide who used it first?

Martin: I'd let Ellie use it first because she's always nice to me.

Mrs Brookes: Very good, Martin. Ellie, if you were in the dinner queue with Megan, and there was only one slice of pizza left, how would you decide who should have it?

Ellie: I'd ask the dinner lady to cut it in half.

Megan: Yes, then we could both have some.

Robbie returns from washing his hands.

Mrs Brookes: Very good. Now, Robbie. Suppose you couldn't find your lunchbox and somebody told you they'd seen Sam with it – what would you do?

Robbie: I'd burn his longhouse down, of course.

Sam: But I haven't got a longhouse.

Megan: Anyway, it's against the law.

Robbie: Oh, all right – I'd take him to the Thing – that's our Viking court – and get him declared an outlaw. **Then** I'd burn his longhouse down …

Mrs Brookes: Oh, dear ... Perhaps we'd better move on to Art.

Martin: I'll get the paper.

Ellie: I'll get the crayons.

Mrs Brookes: Who's going to draw me a nice picture? What are you drawing, Ellie?

Ellie: A squirrel.

Mrs Brookes: Oh, yes – he's nibbling an acorn, isn't he?

Robbie: I like squirrels.

Mrs Brookes: Do you, Robbie?

Robbie: Yes – they're delicious.

Mrs Brookes raises her voice.

Mrs Brookes: Very nice, Ellie. What's this, Sam?

Sam: It's a car.

Mrs Brookes: Oh, so it is.

Sam: It's a Ferrari F355 Berlinetta with a three-and-a-half litre V8 engine …

Mrs Brookes: Yes, thank you, Sam. How about you, Martin?

Martin: I'm drawing a football.

Mrs Brookes: You always draw a football, don't you, Martin?

Martin: I like football. Anyway, footballs are easy to draw, they're round …

Mrs Brookes: Yes, all right. And what about you, Megan?

Megan: I'm drawing a super nuclear-powered spaceship shooting at aliens.

Mrs Brookes: Lovely. And what's this, Robbie? I can't quite see …

Robbie: It's a Viking hero and his defeated enemies.

Mrs Brookes: Oh, yes … Oh, dear … I feel quite ill … Perhaps Art wasn't such a good idea after all.

Robbie: Is this all you do at school? Art, a lot of talking and Maths?

Mrs Brookes: Well, if it's a sunny day outside, we also play games ...

Martin: Oh, yeah! Great idea, Miss.

Sam throws a rugby ball.

Sam: Catch, Robbie!

Martin: Here I come. Rugby tackle!

Robbie: Wow! This is brilliant!

Megan:	To me, Robbie!
Robbie:	It's even more violent than our Viking games!
Mrs Brookes:	Not in here! Mind the windows! Go on, out you go!

The pupils rush out, passing the ball.

| Mrs Brookes: | Oh dear. Oh dear. Coffee, that's what I need. And a biscuit. And a holiday! |

Robbie's Birthday

Characters

Robbie Ravenbeak

a Viking boy

Thor Ravenbeak

Robbie's dad

Freya Ravenbeak

Robbie's mum

Ellie

Martin

Megan

Megan: So this is Robbie's house.

Martin: It's very ... nice.

Ellie: It's got spears and shields all over the walls!

Martin: Well? Your dad's got his snooker trophies in a big glass cabinet. It's practically the same thing.

Megan: Yes, and I didn't hear Robbie complain about those when he came to **your** party.

Ellie: He was too busy stuffing his face with cake.

Robbie, Thor and Freya enter.

Thor: Welcome to Robbie's birthday party!

Freya: Yes, welcome! We have prepared some wonderful party food. Tell them, Robbie.

Robbie: Weeell – we're having raw whale meat and seal blubber sandwiches …

Freya: With puffin nuggets and seagull drumsticks …

Ellie is horrified.

Ellie: I think I'm going to be sick!

Thor: And lots of mead and ale to drink!

Martin: I'm sorry, we're not allowed to drink ale.

Megan: We're not old enough.

Freya: Oh dear – well, I think I've got some nice walrus milk somewhere …

Ellie: I feel even more sick. Just water for me, thanks.

Thor: Time for some musical entertainment!

Martin and Ellie whisper to each other.

Martin: I wonder what sort of music we're having?

Ellie: Perhaps he's got a CD of "Top Viking Tunes"!

Thor strums a harp.

Thor: I will now sing a praise poem about how I built a top-of-the-range longboat from scratch.

Robbie: Oh, Dad, do you have to?

Thor sings.

Thor: Sails shone in the shimmering sunrise
As I happily hammered the planks into place,
Until thwack! I thumped my thumb with
   the hammer
And hopped up and down like a hamster ...
Um – yeah – check it out now ...

Freya: Beautiful! It brings tears to my eyes …

Megan: I bet it brought tears to **his** eyes, too.

Robbie: He always does this – it's so embarrassing.

Thor: Have you seen Robbie's birthday presents?

Freya: We got him a new helmet.

Ellie: Lovely. We've brought presents too, Robbie.

Megan: I've brought you a space rocket filled with soap.

Thor: What's a space rocket?

Robbie: What's soap?

Megan: You know – the stuff you use when you take a bath.

Freya: What's a bath?

Martin quickly interrupts.

Martin: And I've bought you a potato face kit. His ears and nose are detachable, see?

Robbie: So you can chop them off! Brilliant!

Martin: I'm not sure that's exactly the idea …

Ellie: And I've brought you something, too …

Robbie looks hopeful.

Robbie: Gold? Treasure?

Ellie: No – it's a globe.

Robbie: What's it for?

Ellie: It shows you what the world looks like.

Freya: But the world isn't round, it's flat.

Thor: And it has a giant snake swimming around it with its tail in its mouth. Everybody knows that.

Robbie looks disappointed.

Robbie: Oh – well, thanks, anyway.

Freya: What shall we do now?

Thor: I could sing again …

Robbie quickly makes another suggestion.

Robbie: Maybe we could play a game?

Thor: All right – how about 'Pin the Tail on the Dragon'?

Freya: Good idea.

Freya goes out.

Ellie: Don't you mean, 'Pin the Tail on the Donkey'?

Thor: Where's the fun in that?

(He shouts off stage.)

FREYA! IS THAT DRAGON READY YET?

Ellie: What's all that smoke and roaring? Is the kitchen on fire?

Martin: You mean it's a **real** dragon?

From offstage, Freya is heard.

Freya: Naughty dragon! Get down!

Thor: I'll give you a hand!

(He goes out.)

Bad dragon! Stay!

Robbie: I'm sorry – Mum and Dad insisted I had a proper Viking birthday party. I used to like seal blubber and praise songs and all that stuff, but now … It's awful, isn't it?

Ellie: Oh, it's not so bad ...

Megan: Yes it is! It's the worst birthday party I've ever been to!

Ellie: Don't worry, I've got an idea.

Thor and Freya come back.

Thor: We'd better give the dragon a few minutes to calm down.

Ellie: Never mind! I know a good game.

Freya: How do you play it?

Martin: We blindfold you and Mr Ravenbeak, and you have to find us.

Thor: That sounds like fun.

Robbie: I'll do the blindfolds!

Robbie blindfolds his mum and dad. They grope around trying to find the kids.

Ellie whispers.

Ellie: Right! Come on, Robbie. We're off.

Robbie: Where to?

Martin: Fastfood King! They've got a special birthday meal deal.

Megan: You get a pizza, a drink and an ice cream.

Robbie: No raw whalemeat sandwiches? No praise poems from my dad? No dragons?

Ellie: Er – sorry, no.

Martin: You get a sparkler in the ice cream.

Megan: And a paper hat. And a party squeaker.

Robbie heads for the door.

Robbie: Excellent – what are we waiting for? That sounds like a proper birthday party!